Prayer Shawl Quilts™

PRAYER SHAWL QUILTING

For those of us who love to quilt, every quilt we make for family and friends is an act of love. With every stitch, we are thinking about the person who will receive the quilt.

There are times when a special quilt is required to fill a need, provide comfort or give someone a blessing. On such occasions, we need to let those friends, or even strangers, know that we have been praying for them.

Prayer shawls originally were shawls that were knitted or crocheted, but quilters want to share their talent with those in need, too. It is for that reason that we present this collection of throws and lap quilts from designers who have a variety of faith backgrounds.

Contents

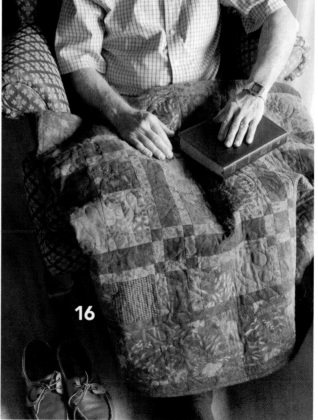

Creating a Prayer Shawl Quilt

When selecting fabric for a prayer shawl quilt, choose 100 percent cotton in a color or a design that will be pleasing to the recipient. Wash and iron the fabric before you start the quilt, so part of the stiffness of the fabric will be removed.

Choose a batting that is washable and does not need to be quilted closer than 6 inches. Because these quilts are meant to be snuggled in, you will want to quilt them as loosely as possible, especially if you machine-quilt them. In many cases, the more quilting you add, the stiffer the quilt will become.

As you begin to stitch the quilt, think about the recipient and how much you love and care for them. Give thanks that you have been blessed with the talent to make a gift that will give them comfort and joy.

After you have given thanks, think of the person for whom you are making the quilt. Let the love you feel for him or her fill your heart and mind; then begin to pray for that person. With each stitch you make, continue to pray for the needs of that person and ask God to bless that person. See the section on prayers beginning on page 4.

GIVING A PRAYER SHAWL QUILT

Many churches with prayer shawl ministries have a special time for presenting these gifts of love to the recipients. Whether you are part of a special prayer shawl group or are making a quilt on your own to give to someone in need, consider this time of presentation as an opportunity to give a blessing or say a prayer verbally with the recipient.

To help you with this presentation, we've added a special section of prayers and blessings and also listed prayers with each item. Select the prayer or blessing that will bring the most comfort and joy to the person. You may want to use a fabric pen to write a prayer or blessing on the label that you add to the back of the quilt.

Prayers and Blessings

FOR SOMEONE WHO TRAVELS

Lord, You are with us everywhere. What a blessing to know that You will travel with us no matter where we go. Give protection and safety as this one travels near or far.

FOR SOMEONE WHO IS MOVING AWAY

Lord, miles are going to separate us as these dear ones are moving away, but we will never be separated from You. So remind us that the same sun is shining on both of us, and distance does not end friendship.

FOR THE DISTRESSED

Lord, sometimes stress overwhelms us, and it seems we have no place to turn. Open Your arms as we flee to You; be our tower of strength. Help us to live one day at a time with Your wisdom and in Your peace.

FOR A NEW BIRTH

Lord, You are the giver of life. Thank You for this new life, this little one who will be loved and cared for in this home. What a special privilege. Bless this family abundantly.

FOR A GRADUATE

Lord, another milestone is here. As graduates, the familiar is behind them, and the unknown stretches out before them. May their skills be sharpened and used. May their knowledge continue to grow, and God's wisdom be theirs as they pursue their dreams.

FOR HEALING

As the Healer of every ill, we come to You and ask for a release from pain, for all the hurts that have been endured and for the gift of healing. Touch this one and bring peace and healing to her soul.

FOR WELCOMING SOMEONE TO YOUR NEIGHBORHOOD, CHURCH, FAMILY

How special to have _____ join us. Lord, You also have precious thoughts about this dear one. Grant us Your joy as we walk and talk together.

FOR A FRIEND

How wonderful to know you are my friend! I thank God for our friendship. God bless you abundantly.

FOR PEACE

Lord, sometimes it seems like there is so much

turmoil and noise around me and within me. Grant me Your peace; fill me with Your peace; surround me with Your peace, blessed peace.

Isaiah 26:3. Lord, You will give me perfect peace when I focus only on You. Lord, I am going to trust You for Your peace.

FOR A LOVED ONE

Lord, You know how special this person is to me and how much I love her. She is also special to You; therefore, I can entrust her to Your care.

FOR COMFORT

Lord, You are my shepherd and You are here to comfort me as You tenderly care for me.

FOR HOPE

When all we see is broken pieces and nothing fits together anymore. When the storms of life have tossed us to and fro, may we find a refuge in Thee. Plant a seed of hope and water it, that it may grow until hope will fill our whole being.

FOR COMFORT

Give _____ the comfort she needs to face the days and hours ahead.

FOR HEALING

You are the God of the impossible. We ask for healing and for hope for the future. Help us to lean on Your strength. Give us Your peace.

FOR HOPE

You came and walked beside us. Help us to lean on Your everlasting arms, to draw strength and hope for the future. Help us to share Your love with those around us and especially with _____.

FOR GUIDANCE

Grant _____ the wisdom, humility and patience she needs as she faces this difficult situation.

FOR A CHILD

May this child live a life of love and share that love with those around him.

May this child always be strong and courageous in his character and in his actions. Help him to do what is right and just and fair.

Grant that this child will learn responsibility, for each one should carry his own load.

Father, teach this child the secret of being content in every situation. Help him to live a life of thankfulness.

Help this baby to be healthy and strong.

FOR MARRIAGE

As these two individuals join their lives together, I ask that You guide them into oneness of life as husband and wife, with each one looking at the other as chosen by God. Wrap them in Your arms in times of distress and give them the courage to say, "I'm sorry," when they are wrong. May they look to You for comfort, strength and wisdom.

Send Your spirit to melt away all fears in this time of need and grant the comfort and love that comes only from You.

Bless this couple as they celebrate their marriage. May they continue to realize the importance of family and fun times. Help their love for each other to grow deeper and to sustain them in times of difficulty.

BLESSINGS
Thank You for bringing _____ our way. May his life be happy and his business prosperous. May he be a blessing to us and may we be a blessing to him.

Father God, bless our work. Let all we do today be for Your glory.

Bless this child. Help him to grow and thrive in a way that would honor his parents and his God. Help him to know love and to share his love with those around him.

Bless this quilt. Make it a comfort and a blessing to the person who receives it. May she find peace during this time of sorrow as she wraps herself in Your love and in this prayer shawl quilt.

Thank You that the act of stitching a prayer shawl quilt has been a blessing to the stitcher. Help it to be a blessing to the person who receives the quilt as well.

QUILTER'S PRAYER OF THANKFULNESS
Thank You for blessing me with the ability to quilt. Thank You for the joy, peace and blessing it brings into my life. It is a gift that has brought me countless hours of pleasure and enjoyment. Father, I return this gift to You. Use this talent to serve Your purpose in the world. Bless each item I quilt so that it radiates Your love to the person who will receive it.

May these roses bring fragrant memories to mind as you travel with a new set of wheels,
with pockets full of love, peace and hope.

Pockets Full of Roses

By Betty Alderman

PROJECT SPECIFICATIONS
Skill Level: Beginner
Quilt Size: 37" x 37"
Block Size: 8" x 8"
Number of Blocks: 9

INSTRUCTIONS
Completing the Blocks
1. Fold each B square in half on one diagonal and press to make a crease.

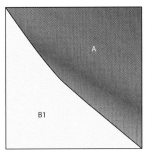

Pocket Full of Roses
8" x 8" Block
Make 9

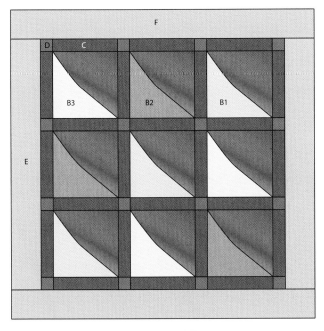

Pockets Full of Roses
Placement Diagram
37" x 37"

FABRIC Measurements based on 42" usable fabric width.	#STRIPS & PIECES	CUT	#PIECES	SUBCUT
⅛ yard coral print	1	2" x 42"	16	2" D squares
⅜ yard cream floral tonal	1	8½" x 42"	3	8½" B3 squares
⅜ yard light gold tonal	1	8½" x 42"	3	8½" B1 squares
⅜ yard gold/ metallic print	1	8½" x 42"	3	8½" B2 squares
½ yard rose plaid	6	2" x 42"	24	8½" C strips
⅝ yard tan tonal	2 / 2	4" x 30½" E / 4" x 37½" F		
1⅛ yards rose floral	3 / 4	8½" x 42" / 2¼" x 42" binding	9	8½" A squares
Backing		43" x 43"		

SUPPLIES
- Batting 43" x 43"
- All-purpose thread to match fabric
- Quilting thread
- Basic sewing tools and supplies

2. Place a folded B square on the left side of one A square, matching corners referring to the block drawing; machine-baste to hold B in place along the two matched raw edges as shown in Figure 1 to complete one Pocket Full of Roses block. Repeat to complete nine blocks—three each using B1, B2 and B3 squares.

Figure 1

Completing the Quilt

1. Arrange the completed blocks in three rows of three blocks and four C strips each referring to the Placement Diagram for positioning of B pieces; join in rows. Press seams toward C strips.

2. Join three C strips with four D squares to make a sashing row; press seams toward D. Repeat to make four sashing rows.

3. Join the sashing rows with the block rows referring to the Placement Diagram for positioning of block rows; press seams toward sashing rows.

4. Sew an E strip to opposite sides and F strips to the top and bottom to complete the pieced top; press seams toward E and F strips.

5. Sandwich the batting between the completed top and prepared backing; pin or baste layers together to hold.

6. Quilt as desired by hand or machine; remove pins or basting. Trim excess backing and batting even with quilt top.

7. Join binding strips on short ends to make one long strip. Fold the strip in half along length with wrong sides together; press.

8. Sew binding to quilt edges, mitering corners and overlapping ends. Fold binding to the back side and stitch in place to finish. ∎

Lord God, You are the God of the impossible. We ask for help during this difficult time and for hope for the future. Help us to lean on your strength. Give us your peace. Amen.

Words of Comfort

By Connie Kauffman

PROJECT NOTES

The messages on this quilt can be hand-printed or colored from stencils using permanent fabric markers.

Another method would be to type the words on your computer and print them off in your favorite font to fit the size of the message unit (3" x 9"). Place the printed paper behind the message unit, and trace over the letters with the permanent fabric marker.

It is wise to test the marker by washing a written sample before actually adding messages to the quilt.

PROJECT SPECIFICATIONS

Skill Level: Beginner
Quilt Size: 53" x 62"
Block Size: 9" x 9"
Number of Blocks: 10

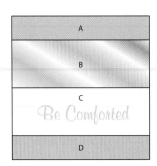

Comfort
9" x 9" Block
Make 10

FABRIC Measurements based on 42" usable fabric width.	#STRIPS & PIECES	CUT	#PIECES	SUBCUT
¼ yard pink/green/white stripe	3	2" x 42" A		
⅜ yard white solid	3	3½" x 42" C		
⅜ yard small floral	3	3½" x 42" B		
⅓ yard purple print	3	1½" x 42" F		
	2	1½" x 38½" G		
⅝ yard trellis print	2	3" x 38½" H		
	3	3" x 42" I		
¾ yard green/white stripe	3	2" x 42" D		
	6	2¼" x 42" binding		
2 yards large floral	2	5½" x 43½" J along length		
	2	5½" x 62½" K along length		
	2	9½" along length	10	9½" E squares
Backing		59" x 68"		

SUPPLIES

- Batting 59" x 68"
- All-purpose thread to match fabric
- Quilting thread
- Teal permanent fabric marker
- Upper- and lowercase script letter stencils
- Basic sewing tools and supplies

INSTRUCTIONS

Completing the Blocks

1. Join one each A, B, C and D strip in alphabetical order to make an A-B-C-D strip set; press seams in one direction. Repeat to make three strip sets.

2. Subcut strip sets into (10) 9½" Comfort blocks as shown in Figure 1.

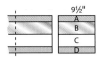

Figure 1

Completing the Quilt

1. Join two Comfort blocks with two E squares to make a row as shown in Figure 2; press seams in one direction. Repeat to make five rows.

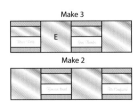

Figure 2

2. Join the rows, alternating rows referring to the Placement Diagram, to complete the pieced center; press seams in one direction.

3. Using letter stencils and permanent fabric markers, trace and color comforting messages in the C areas of each block. *Note: Messages on the sample quilt include the following: Have Faith, Give Thanks, You Are Loved, Be Comforted, Keep Hope Alive, Here's a Hug, Seek Joy, Friends Are Close to Your Heart, Count Your Blessings, and Be Happy.*

4. Join the F strips with right sides together on the short ends to make one long strip; press seams open. Subcut strip into two 45½" F strips.

5. Sew an F strip to opposite long sides and G strips to the top and bottom of the pieced center; press seams toward F and G strips.

6. Sew an H strip to the top and bottom of the pieced center; press seams toward H strips.

7. Join the I strips with right sides together on the short ends to make one long strip; press seams open. Subcut strip into two 52½" I strips.

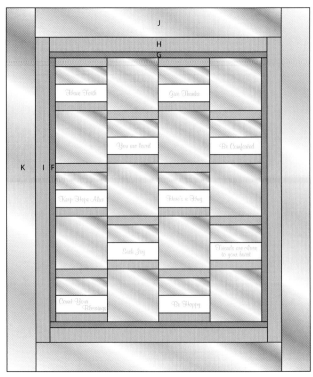

Words of Comfort
Placement Diagram
53" x 62"

8. Sew the I strips to opposite long sides of the pieced center; press seams toward I strips.

9. Sew a J strip to the top and bottom and K strips to opposite long sides to complete the pieced top; press seams toward J and K strips.

10. Sandwich the batting between the completed top and prepared backing; pin or baste layers together to hold.

11. Quilt as desired by hand or machine; remove pins or basting. Trim excess backing and batting even with quilt top.

12. Join binding strips on short ends to make one long strip. Fold the strip in half along length with wrong sides together; press.

13. Sew binding to quilt edges, mitering corners and overlapping ends. Fold binding to the back side and stitch in place to finish. ■

Lord, as I look to the hills, I am reminded that You not only are my maker but also my constant sustainer. You walk with me on the rough path that I am hiking on right now. Amen.

Unending Prayer Ribbons

By Jill Reber

PROJECT SPECIFICATIONS
Skill Level: Beginner
Quilt Size: 42" x 58"
Block Size: 8" x 8"
Number of Blocks: 24

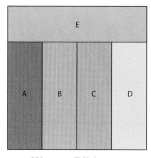

Woven Ribbons
8" x 8" Block
Make 24

FABRIC Measurements based on 42" usable fabric width.		#STRIPS & PIECES	CUT	#PIECES	SUBCUT
	⅜ yard red floral tonal	4	2½" x 42" A		
	⅜ yard green print	4	2½" x 42" B		
	⅜ yard brown tonal	4	2½" x 42" C		
	⅜ yard gold print	4	2½" x 42" D		
	½ yard red tonal	6	2¼" x 42" binding		
	⅝ yard blue print	2	8½" x 42"	24	2½" E rectangles
	1 yard green floral print	2	5½" x 32½" F		
		3	5½" x 42" G		
	Backing		48" x 64"		

SUPPLIES
- Batting 48" x 64"
- All-purpose thread to match fabric
- Quilting thread
- Basic sewing tools and supplies

INSTRUCTIONS
Completing the Blocks
1. Join one each A, B, C and D strips in alphabetical order to make an A-B-C-D strip set; press seams in one direction. Repeat to make four strip sets.

2. Subcut strip sets into (24) 6½" A-B-C-D units as shown in Figure 1.

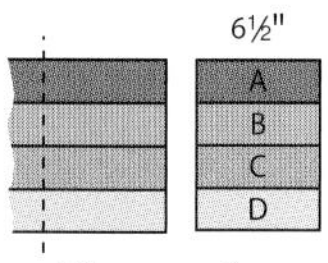

Figure 1

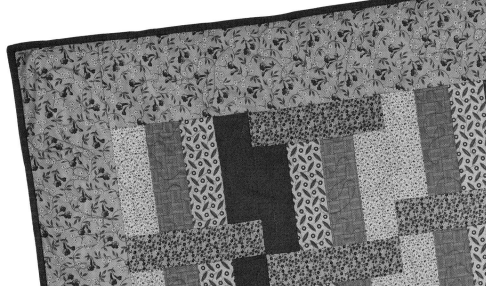

3. Sew E to the top edge of each A-B-C-D unit to complete one Woven Ribbons block as shown in Figure 2; press seam toward E. Repeat to complete 24 Woven Ribbons blocks.

Figure 2

Completing the Quilt

1. Join six blocks to make a vertical row as shown in Figure 3; press seams in one direction. Repeat to make four rows.

Figure 3

2. Join the rows, alternating direction of rows, to complete the pieced center; press seams in one direction.

3. Sew an F strip to the top and bottom of the pieced center; press seams toward F strips.

4. Join the G strips with right sides together on the short ends to make one long strip; press seams open. Subcut strip into two 58½" G strips.

5. Sew a G strip to opposite long sides of the pieced center to complete the pieced top.

6. Sandwich the batting between the completed top and prepared backing; pin or baste layers together to hold.

7. Quilt as desired by hand or machine; remove pins or basting. Trim excess backing and batting even with quilt top.

8. Join binding strips on short ends to make one long strip. Fold the strip in half along length with wrong sides together; press.

9. Sew binding to quilt edges, mitering corners and overlapping ends. Fold binding to the back side and stitch in place to finish. ■

Unending Prayer Ribbons
Placement Diagram
42" x 58"

Lord, we thank you that you are always ready to help. Surround him with your love and grant him peace of mind, peace of heart and peace of soul. Wrap him in your tender care. Amen.

Warm Thoughts Flannel Throw

By Julie Weaver

PROJECT SPECIFICATIONS

Skill Level: Beginner
Quilt Size: 52" x 64"
Block Size: 12" x 12"
Number of Blocks: 12

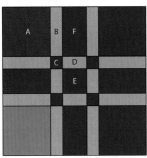

Warm Thoughts
12" x 12" Block
Make 12

FABRIC Measurements based on 42" usable fabric width. All fabrics are flannel.	#STRIPS & PIECES	CUT
48 coordinating 4½" A squares		
⅞ yard gold print	14	1½" x 42" B
	1	2½" x 42" D
1¼ yards animal print	6	6½" x 42" I
1⅔ yards dark blue tonal	2	1½" x 42" C
	1	2½" x 42" E
	6	2½" x 42" F
	11	1½" x 42" G/H/J/K
	6	2¼" x 42" binding
Backing		58" x 70"

SUPPLIES

- Batting 58" x 70"
- All-purpose thread to match fabric
- Quilting thread
- Basic sewing tools and supplies

INSTRUCTIONS

Completing the Blocks

1. Sew an F strip between two B strips with right sides together along length to make a B-F strip set; press seams toward F. Repeat to make six strip sets.

2. Subcut the B-F strip sets into (48) 4½" B-F-B units as shown in Figure 1.

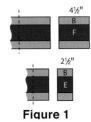

Figure 1

3. Repeat step 1 with B and E strips to make one B-E-B strip set; subcut strip set into (12) 2½" B-E-B units, again referring to Figure 1.

4. Sew a D strip between two C strips with right sides together along length to make a C-D strip set; press seams toward C.

5. Subcut the C-D strip set into (12) 1½" C-D-C units as shown in Figure 2.

6. To complete one Warm Thoughts block, sew a C-D-C unit to opposite sides of a B-E-B unit to complete the center unit as shown in Figure 3; press seams toward the B-E-B unit.

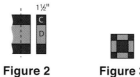

Figure 2   **Figure 3**

7. Sew a B-F-B unit to opposite sides of the center unit to complete the center row as shown in Figure 4; press seams toward the B-F-B unit.

Figure 4   **Figure 5**

8. Select four A squares; sew a B-F-B unit between two A squares to complete the top row as shown in Figure 5; press seams toward the B-F-B unit. Repeat to make the bottom row.

9. Sew the top and bottom rows to the center row referring to the block drawing to complete one Warm Thoughts block; press seams away from the center row.

10. Repeat steps 6–9 to complete 12 Warm Thoughts blocks.

Completing the Quilt
1. Join three blocks to make a row; press seams in one direction. Repeat to make four rows.

2. Join the rows, alternating the direction of the pressed seam allowances, to complete the quilt center; press seams in one direction.

3. Join the G/H/J/K strips with right sides together on short ends to complete one long strip; subcut strip into two each 48½" G strips, 38½" H strips, 62½" J strips and 52½" K strips.

4. Sew a G strip to opposite long sides and H strips to the top and bottom of the pieced center; press seams toward G and H strips.

5. Join the I strips with right sides together on short ends to complete one long strip; subcut strip into four 50½" I strips.

6. Sew an I strip to opposite long sides and to the top and bottom of the pieced center; press seams toward I strips.

7. Sew the J strips to opposite long sides and the K strips to the top and bottom of the pieced center; press seams toward J and K strips.

8. Sandwich the batting between the completed top and prepared backing; pin or baste layers together to hold.

9. Quilt as desired by hand or machine; remove pins or basting. Trim excess backing and batting even with quilt top.

10. Join binding strips on short ends to make one long strip. Fold the strip in half along length with wrong sides together; press.

11. Sew binding to quilt edges, mitering corners and overlapping ends. Fold binding to the back side and stitch in place to finish. ■

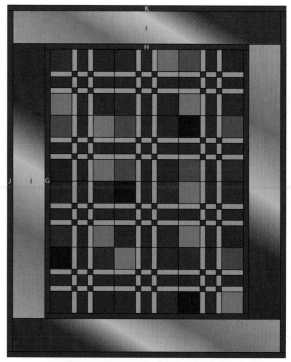

Warm Thoughts Flannel Throw
Placement Diagram
52" x 64"

Lord, You are the great comforter; surround this dear one with loving arms as they grieve. Give them strength and peace to carry on, resting in your sustaining power. Amen.

Floral Lap Quilt

By Barbara Clayton

PROJECT SPECIFICATIONS

Skill Level: Intermediate
Quilt Size: 46¼" x 59"
Block Size: 9" x 9"
Number of Blocks: 18

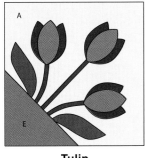

Tulip
9" x 9" Block
Make 12

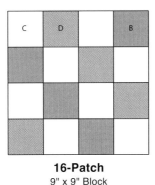

16-Patch
9" x 9" Block
Make 6

INSTRUCTIONS

Completing the Tulip Blocks

1. Trace the appliqué shapes onto the paper side of the freezer paper as directed on patterns for number to cut. **Note:** *To reduce cutting, you may trace the shapes onto one piece of freezer paper and layer with multiple pieces to cut more than one piece at a time. Be sure to pin the layers together to hold for accurate cutting.*

2. Press the waxy side of the freezer-paper shapes to the wrong side of fabrics as directed on pattern for color.

3. Cut out each shape leaving ¼" all around for turn-under seam allowance; clip into curves, points and indentations almost to the paper patterns.

FABRIC Measurements based on 42" usable fabric width.	#STRIPS & PIECES	CUT	#PIECES	SUBCUT
¼ yard medium green print	2	2¾" x 42" B		
¼ yard red/ cream gingham	2 1	2¾" x 42" D 2½" x 42" M		
¼ yard dark green mottled		Appliqué pieces as per patterns		
¼ yard dark green tonal		Appliqué pieces as per patterns		
½ yard cream crackle	4	2¾" x 42" C		
⅝ yard rose mottled	3 2	1½" x 42" H 1½" x 38¾" I Appliqué pieces as per patterns		
¾ yard tan/red print	1	14" x 42"	3	14" squares; cut on both diagonals to make 10 G triangles
	1	7¼" x 42"	2	7¼" squares; cut in half on 1 diagonal to make 4 F triangles
1 yard rose tonal	1 6 2	2½" x 42" L 2¼" x 42" binding 5½" x 42" Appliqué pieces as per patterns	12	5½" E squares
1½ yards cream/ tan print	3 3 2	9½" x 42" 3½" x 42" J 3½" x 38¾" K	12	9½" A squares
Backing		53" x 65"		

SUPPLIES

- Batting 53" x 65"
- All-purpose thread to match fabric
- Quilting thread
- Clear nylon monofilament
- Water-soluble marker
- Water-soluble glue stick
- Freezer paper
- Dinner plate
- Basic sewing tools and supplies

4. Using a glue stick, glue the seam allowance over the edge and to the back of the freezer paper; glue all the way around each piece except for edges marked by dashed gray lines on the pattern.

5. Using the full-size pattern as a guide, pin the appliqué pieces together in numerical order, overlapping pieces as necessary; stitch together along the overlapping edges of each piece with a narrow blind-hem stitch and clear nylon thread.

6. Fold each A square and crease to mark the diagonal centers.

7. To complete one Tulip block, center one tulip motif on one A square in numerical order referring to Figure 1 for positioning; stitch in place as in step 5.

Figure 1

8. Mark a diagonal line from corner to corner on the wrong side of each E square.

9. Referring to Figure 2, place E right sides together on the bottom corner of A; stitch on the marked line. Trim seam to ¼" and press E to the right side to complete one block.

Figure 2

10. Repeat steps 7–9 to complete 12 Tulip blocks.

11. Turn each block wrong side up and make a slit behind the flower and leaf shapes; trim away the backing to ¼" from the edge of the stitching around the shapes.

12. Use a sponge or cloth to wet the back of each shape. Tear away the freezer paper from behind each shape; let dry and press lightly.

Completing the 16-Patch Blocks

1. Sew a B strip to a C strip with right sides together along length; press seams toward B. Repeat to make two B-C strip sets.

2. Subcut the B-C strip sets into (24) 2¾" B-C units as shown in Figure 3.

Figure 3

3. Repeat steps 1 and 2 with D and C strips to complete 24 D-C units.

4. To complete one 16-Patch block, join one each B-C and D-C units to make a row as shown in Figure 4; press seams in one direction. Repeat to make four rows.

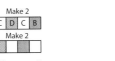

Figure 4   **Figure 5**

5. Join the rows, alternating every other one referring to Figure 5 to complete one 16-Patch block; press seams in one direction.

6. Repeat steps 4 and 5 to complete six 16-Patch blocks.

Completing the Quilt

1. Arrange and join the Tulip and 16-Patch blocks with F and G triangles in diagonal rows to complete the pieced center as shown in Figure 6; press seams away from Tulip blocks.

Figure 6

2. Join the H strips with right sides together on short ends to make one long strip; press seams open. Subcut strip into two 51½" H strips. Repeat to make two same-length J strips.

3. Sew an H strip to a J strip with right sides together along length; press seams toward H. Repeat to make two H-J strips. Repeat with I and K strips to make two I-K strips.

4. Sew an H-J strip to opposite sides of the pieced center referring to the Placement Diagram for positioning of strips; press seams toward the H-J strips.

5. Sew the L strip to the M strip with right sides together along the length; press seams toward M.

6. Subcut the L-M strip set into eight 2½" L-M units as shown in Figure 7.

Figure 7   **Figure 8**

7. Join two L-M units to complete a corner unit as shown in Figure 8; press seam in one direction.

8. Sew an L-M unit to each end of each I-K strip referring to Figure 9; press seams toward I-K strips.

Figure 9

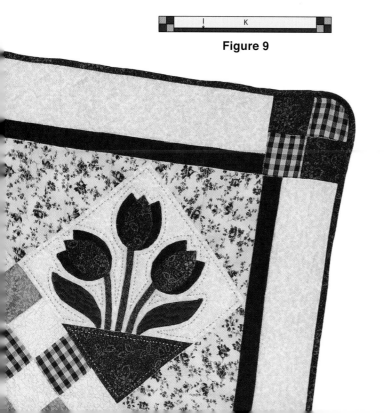

Floral Lap Quilt
Placement Diagram
46¼" x 59"

9. Sew the I-K/L-M strips to the top and bottom of the pieced center to complete the top; press seams toward the I-K/L-M strips.

10. Sandwich the batting between the completed top and prepared backing; pin or baste layers together to hold.

11. Quilt as desired by hand or machine; remove pins or basting. Trim excess backing and batting even with quilt top.

12. Use a dinner plate to round each corner.

13. Join binding strips on short ends to make one long strip. Fold the strip in half along length with wrong sides together; press.

14. Sew binding to quilt edges, mitering corners and overlapping ends. Fold binding to the back side and stitch in place to finish. ■

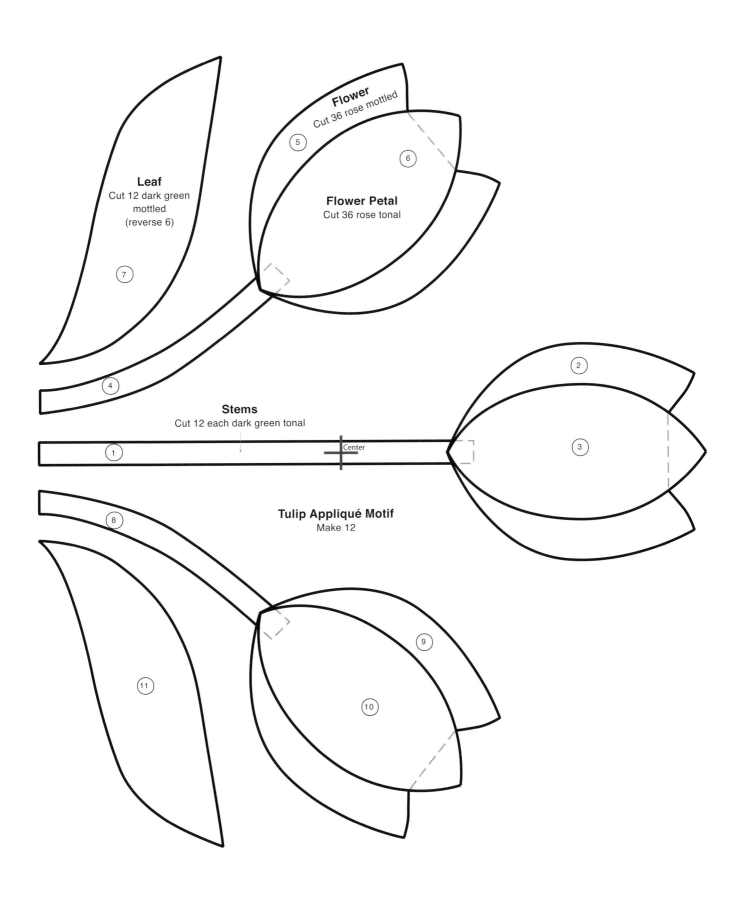

Leaf
Cut 12 dark green mottled (reverse 6)

Flower
Cut 36 rose mottled

Flower Petal
Cut 36 rose tonal

Stems
Cut 12 each dark green tonal

Center

Tulip Appliqué Motif
Make 12

As God's tender care is sufficient for the lilies of the field, may His tender care watch over you as well. May God wrap his arms of love around you, even as you wrap this shawl about you.

Calla Lily Shawl

By Jodi Warner

PROJECT SPECIFICATIONS
Skill Level: Advanced
Shawl Size: 14½" x 65"

INSTRUCTIONS

Completing the Lily Units

1. Make copies of the lily paper-piecing patterns as directed with patterns.

2. Cut up one copy of each pattern to make individual patterns for each piece; add at least ¼" all around each piece and use to rough-cut pieces from fabrics as directed.

3. Place piece 1 right side up on the unmarked side of one paper copy, covering the piece 1 section and extending at least ¼" into all surrounding sections. Place piece 2 right sides together with piece 1 on the 1-2 seam side as shown in Figure 1; turn paper over and stitch on the marked 1-2 line.

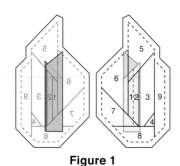

Figure 1

FABRIC Measurements based on 42" usable fabric width.	#STRIPS & PIECES	CUT	#PIECES	SUBCUT
Cream, light tan and dark tan scraps		See paper-piecing patterns		
¼ yard medium green tonal		Leaf pieces as per pattern		
¼ yard dark purple print	2	1" x 42"	4	7" P pieces
			2	12" Q pieces
	3	1" x 42" O		
⅓ yard light green tonal	6	¾" x 42"	2	22" N strips
			4	25" M strips
			2	4¾" D pieces
			2	5¼" E pieces
			2	6" H pieces
			2	6½" I pieces
	1	2" x 42"	4	2" K squares
1½ yards medium violet tonal	1	4¾" x 42"	1	4¾" C square
			2	3½" x 8¼" B pieces
			2	⅞" x 5¼" F pieces
			2	⅞" x 6" G pieces
	1	7⅝" x 42"	2	7⅝" squares; cut in half on 1 diagonal to make 4 J triangles
	1	14" x 42"	2	20½" L strips
	5	2¼" x 42" binding A and AR pieces as per template		
Backing		20" x 71"		

SUPPLIES
- Batting 20" x 71"
- All-purpose thread to match fabric
- Quilting thread
- Basic sewing tools and supplies

4. Trim excess seam to ¼"; press piece 2 to the right side as shown in Figure 2.

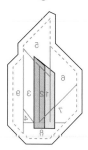

Figure 2

5. Continue adding pieces in numerical order in this manner until entire paper foundation is covered.

6. Trim finished foundation along outside-edge line to complete a lily unit.

7. Repeat steps 3–6 to complete four lily and two reverse lily units.

8. Remove paper from each lily and reverse lily unit.

9. Turn under the edges of each lily and reverse lily unit ¼"; baste to hold.

Preparing the Stem Pieces

1. Position two pins 3" apart on your ironing surface to form a ¼"-wide channel through which to press the M and N strips as shown in Figure 3.

2. Fold the long edges of one M strip under ¼" and thread through the pinned channel on the ironing board cover as shown in Figure 4; press with tip of iron. Continue turning and pulling the strip through the channel while pressing to press the entire strip. Repeat for all M and N strips. *Note: The pinned channel helps keep the width of the strips uniform and keeps fingers safe from being burned by the iron.*

Figure 3   **Figure 4**

Completing the End Panels

1. To complete one end panel, position and baste a completed lily unit on B referring to Figure 5; hand-stitch in place all around to complete the B unit, leaving open the bottom center to insert the N piece later.

Figure 5

2. Position and baste the remaining lily on AR and the reverse lily on A referring to Figure 6 and the A/AR pattern for positioning; hand-stitch in place all around except for the bottom centers of the lily units, which are left open to insert M stem pieces.

   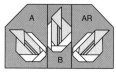

Figure 6   **Figure 7**

3. Sew the B unit between the A and AR units to complete one end panel as shown in Figure 7; press seams away from the center B unit. Repeat steps 1–3 to complete two end panels.

Completing the Center Block

1. Sew D to opposite sides and E to the remaining sides of C as shown in Figure 8; press seams toward D and E.

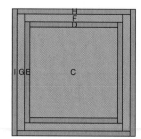

Figure 8

2. Repeat step 1 with F, G, H and I pieces to complete the center unit; press seams away from the center after adding each strip.

3. Align and match the seam-allowance corner of J with the seam-allowance corner of the pieced

center unit as shown in Figure 9; stitch to the opposite end of the center unit, leaving J excess extending. Press seam away from J.

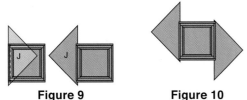

Figure 9   **Figure 10**

4. Repeat step 3 with J on the opposite side of the center unit as shown in Figure 10.

5. Trim excess J even with the center unit as shown in Figure 11.

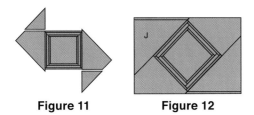

Figure 11   **Figure 12**

6. Sew J to the remaining sides of the pieced J/center unit to complete the center panel as shown in Figure 12; press seams toward J.

Completing the Quilt
1. Fold and crease each L piece to mark the lengthwise center.

2. Sew L to opposite sides of the center panel and add the end panels referring to the Placement Diagram for positioning; press seams toward L.

3. Turn under the edges of each K square ¼" all around; baste to hold.

4. Center a corner of each K square at each corner point of the center unit referring to the Placement Diagram; baste to hold in place.

5. Center and hand-stitch an N strip along the creased line on each L piece, under the corner of K and into the opening left in the bottom of the center lily on the B unit referring to the Placement Diagram for positioning.

6. Arrange and stitch an M strip on each side of N aligning ends of M at the corners of K, folding M strips at the seam between A or AR and L to angle strip toward A and AR, and inserting ends in opening left on the bottom of each side lily on A and AR as shown in Figure 13.

Figure 13

7. Hand-stitch K squares in place over the ends of N and M and at the points of the center unit in the center panel.

8. Trace leaf shapes onto the right side of the leaf fabric as directed on pattern for number and color to cut. Cut out shapes and turn under edges on traced lines; baste to hold.

9. Position and baste three leaf shapes on each L piece with upper leaf approximately 8" below the center lily block and angled at approximately 45 degrees as shown in Figure 14. Position remaining leaves at similar angles approximately ⅝" apart with second leaf pointing opposite the top leaf and third leaf pointing in the same direction as the top leaf, again referring to Figure 14; hand-stitch in place to complete the top.

Figure 14

10. Join O strips with right sides together on short ends to make one long strip; press seams open. Subcut strip into two 61" O strips.

11. Center and sew O strips to opposite long sides of the completed center; press seams toward O strips. Trim ends at the same angle as the end panels using a straightedge as shown in Figure 15.

Figure 15

12. Add P strips to angled edges and Q strips to ends of the completed center, trimming as in step 11 to complete the pieced top.

13. Mark the top for quilting using leaf and center patterns given, positioning leaf pattern ⅝" from O outer border edges on the center panel and L as shown in Figure 16.

Figure 16

Calla Lily Prayer Shawl
Placement Diagram
14½" x 65"

14. Sandwich the batting between the completed top and prepared backing; pin or baste layers together to hold.

15. Quilt on marked lines and as desired by hand or machine; remove pins or basting. Trim excess backing and batting even with quilt top.

16. Join binding strips on short ends to make one long strip. Fold the strip in half along length with wrong sides together; press.

17. Sew binding to quilt edges, mitering corners and overlapping ends. Fold binding to the back side and stitch in place to finish. ■

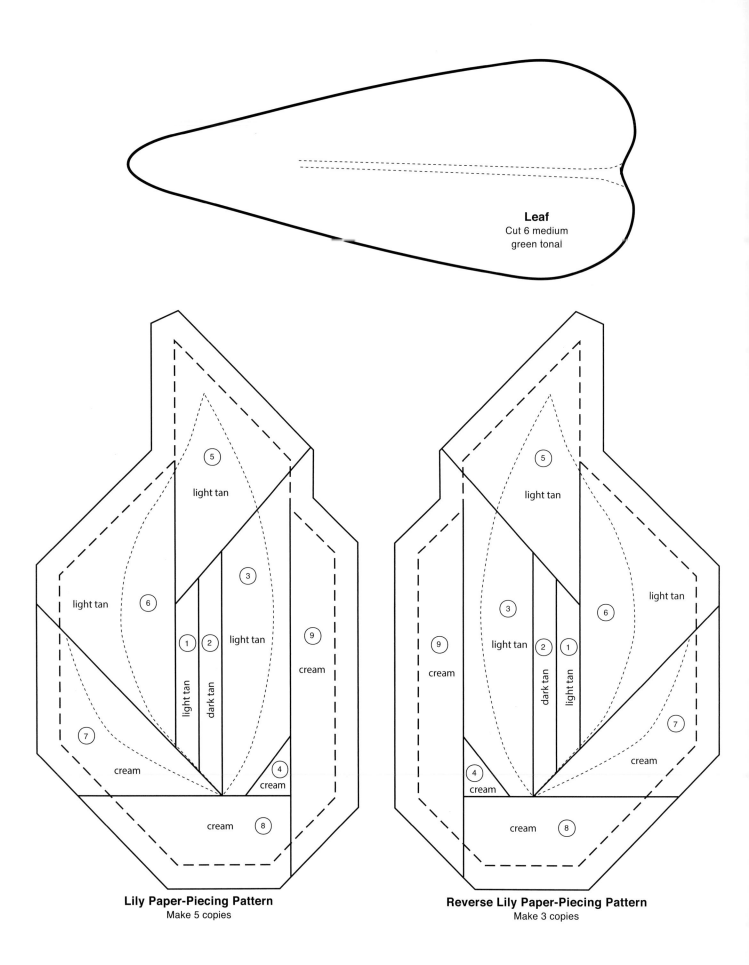

Leaf
Cut 6 medium
green tonal

Lily Paper-Piecing Pattern
Make 5 copies

Reverse Lily Paper-Piecing Pattern
Make 3 copies

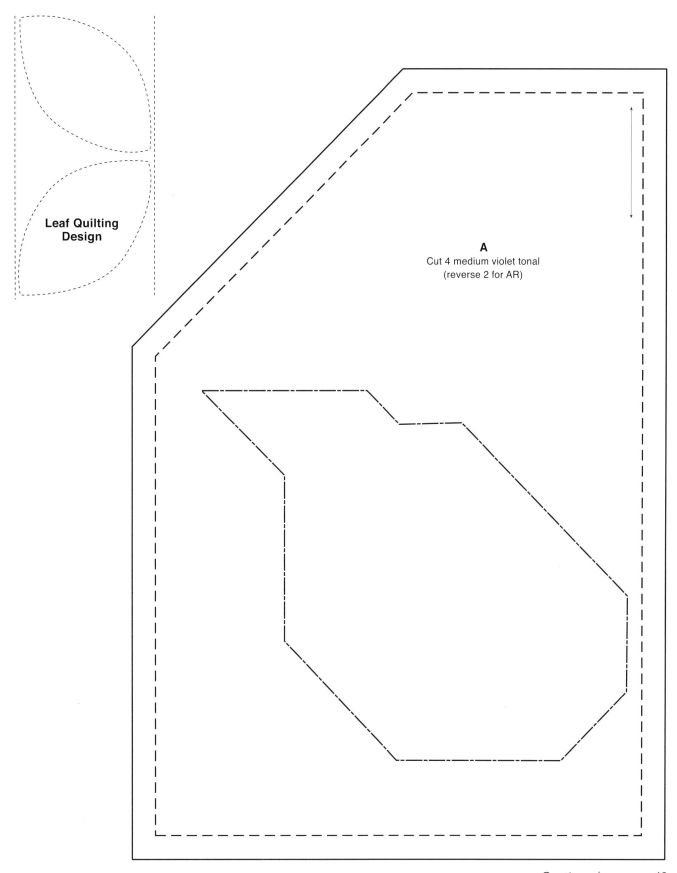

Leaf Quilting Design

A
Cut 4 medium violet tonal
(reverse 2 for AR)

Continued on page 48.

Ribbons of Hope

By Connie Kauffman

PROJECT SPECIFICATIONS

Skill Level: Beginner
Quilt Size: 54" x 64"
Block Size: 5" x 5"
Number of Blocks: 80

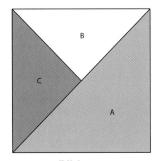

Ribbons
5" x 5" Block
Make 80

FABRIC Measurements based on 42" usable fabric width.	#STRIPS & PIECES	CUT	#PIECES	SUBCUT
10 light pink fat quarters	4	5⅞" squares each fabric		Cut in half on 1 diagonal to make 4 A triangles each fabric
10 dark pink fat quarters	2	6¼" squares each fabric		Cut on both diagonals to make 8 C triangles each fabric
		2¼" x 21" strips to total 250" for binding		
½ yard dark pink tonal	5	2½" x 42" D/E		
⅞ yard white tonal	4	6¼" x 42"	20	6¼" squares; cut on both diagonals to make 80 B triangles
1⅛ yards pink check	6	5½" x 42" F		
Backing		60" x 70"		

SUPPLIES

- Batting 60" x 70"
- All-purpose thread to match fabric
- Quilting thread
- Basic sewing tools and supplies

INSTRUCTIONS

Completing the Blocks

1. Select eight each matching A and matching C triangles.

2. Sew C to B to complete a B-C unit as shown in Figure 1; press seam toward C.

Figure 1

3. Add A to the B-C unit to complete one Ribbon block referring to the block drawing; press seams toward A.

4. Repeat steps 1–3 to make eight matching Ribbon blocks. Repeat to make 10 sets of eight blocks.

Completing the Quilt

1. Join eight matching blocks to make an X row as shown in Figure 2; press seams in one direction. Repeat to make five X rows.

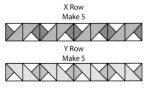

X Row
Make 5

Y Row
Make 5

Figure 2

2. Repeat step 1 with eight matching blocks to make a Y row, again referring to Figure 2; press seams in one direction. Repeat to make five Y rows.

3. Alternate and join the X and Y rows to complete the pieced center referring to Figure 3 and the Placement Diagram; press seams in one direction.

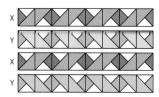

Figure 3

4. Join the D-E strips with right sides together on short ends to make one long strip; press seams open. Subcut strip into two 50½" D strips and two 44½" E strips.

5. Sew the D strips to opposite long sides and E strips to the top and bottom of the pieced center; press seams toward D and E strips.

6. Join the F strips with right sides together on short ends to make one long strip; press

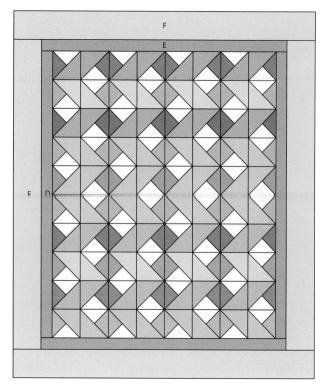

Ribbons of Hope
Placement Diagram
54" x 64"

seams open. Subcut strip into four 54½" F strips.

7. Sew the F strips to opposite long sides and to the top and bottom of the pieced center; press seams toward F strips to complete the top.

8. Sandwich the batting between the completed top and prepared backing; pin or baste layers together to hold.

9. Quilt as desired by hand or machine; remove pins or basting. Trim excess backing and batting even with quilt top.

10. Join binding strips on short ends to make one long strip. Fold the strip in half along length with wrong sides together; press.

11. Sew binding to quilt edges, mitering corners and overlapping ends. Fold binding to the back side and stitch in place to finish. ∎

Dear little one, may this guardian angel watch over you night and day. May he spread his wings over you to protect you, beneath you to carry you, beside you as a friend, and around you as a cloud of love.

Guardian Angel Baby Quilt

By Chris Malone

PROJECT SPECIFICATIONS

Skill Level: Intermediate
Quilt Size: 43" x 49"
Block Size: 9" x 9" and 12" x 12"
Number of Blocks: 18 and 3

FABRIC Measurements based on 44" usable fabric width.	#STRIPS & PIECES	CUT
Peach, rose, burgundy, gold, green and white scraps		Appliqué pieces as directed on patterns
9—6" x 6" scraps yellow solids or tonals	2 1	2⅞" E squares each scrap 2½" C square each scrap
9 fat quarters light–medium blue prints or tonals	81 24 4 2	2½" A squares total 6½" B squares total 2½" F squares each fabric 2⅞" D squares each fabric
½ yard medium blue print	5	2¼" x 44" binding
⅝ yard dark blue tonal	2 2	4" x 42½" G 4" x 43½" H
Backing		49" x 55"

Angel With Horn
12" x 12" Block
Make 1

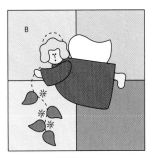

Angel With Leaves
12" x 12" Block
Make 1

Nine-Patch
6" x 6" Block
Make 9

Angel With Heart
12" x 12" Block
Make 1

Star
6" x 6" Block
Make 9

SUPPLIES

- Batting 49" x 55"
- All-purpose thread to match fabric
- Quilting thread
- Medium blue, dark rose, dark yellow, green and white embroidery floss
- ¾ yard 12"-wide lightweight fusible web
- Scrap lightweight fusible interfacing (optional)
- Air-soluble marker
- Basic sewing tools and supplies

INSTRUCTIONS

Completing the Nine-Patch Blocks

1. To complete one Nine-Patch block, join three A squares to make a row; press seams in one direction. Repeat to make three rows.

2. Join the rows with seams in alternating directions to complete one block; press seams in one direction.

3. Repeat steps 1 and 2 to complete nine Nine-Patch blocks.

Completing the Star Blocks

1. Mark a diagonal line from corner to corner on the wrong side of each D square.

2. Place an E square right sides together with a D square and stitch ¼" on each side of the marked line referring to Figure 1; cut apart on the marked line and press open with seam toward E to complete a D-E unit. Repeat to make 36 D-E units.

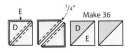

Figure 1

3. To complete one Star block, select four each matching D-E units and F squares and one matching C square.

Guardian Angel Baby Quilt
Placement Diagram
43" x 49"

4. Sew an F square to opposite sides of one D-E unit to make the top row as shown in Figure 2; press seams toward F. Repeat to make the bottom row.

Figure 2

Figure 3

5. Sew a D-E unit to opposite sides of C to complete the center row as shown in Figure 3; press seams toward C.

6. Join the rows referring to the block drawing to complete one Star block; press seams in one direction.

7. Repeat steps 3–6 to complete nine Star blocks.

Completing the Angel Blocks

1. To complete one Angel With Leaves block, select four B squares. Join two squares to make a row; press seam to one side. Repeat to make two rows.

2. Join the rows to complete a B unit as shown in Figure 4; press seam in one direction.

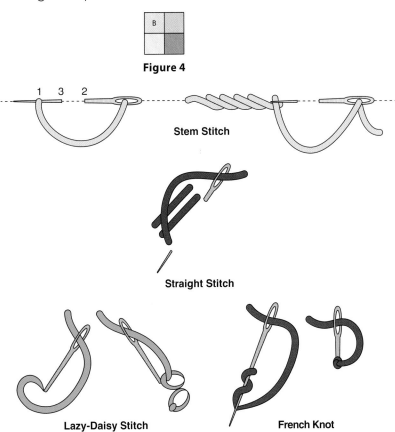

Figure 4

Stem Stitch

Straight Stitch

Lazy-Daisy Stitch   French Knot

3. Trace all angel pattern pieces onto the paper side of the lightweight fusible web as directed on patterns; cut out shapes, leaving a margin around each one.

4. To reduce stiffness and bulk on larger pieces, cut out the center part of the dress, sleeve and wing pieces by cutting ¼" inside the pattern lines.

5. Fuse shapes to the wrong side of fabrics. **Note:** *If white and peach fabrics are too transparent, fuse lightweight fusible interfacing to the wrong side of these fabrics before adding the fusible web.* Cut out shapes on marked lines.

6. Arrange and fuse the shapes onto the B unit in numerical order, matching centerlines on the angel motif with the center seam of the B unit.

7. Using thread to match fabrics and a machine blanket stitch, sew around each shape.

8. Transfer the vine pattern to the block with the air-soluble marker; use 2 strands of green floss to embroider a stem stitch on the marked line.

9. For each flower, make eight lazy-daisy stitches around a center point with 2 strands white floss. Make a French knot with 4 strands of dark yellow floss for each flower center.

10. Transfer facial features and halo to the block with the air-soluble marker. Use 2 strands of blue floss to make French knot eyes, dark rose French knots for mouth and dark yellow to stem-stitch halo. Make a straight stitch down the center of the face for the nose with 1 strand of dark rose floss to complete the block.

11. Repeat steps 1–10 as needed to complete one Angel With Horn and one Angel With Heart blocks, placing horn and heart shapes under the hands before applying hands to the B unit.

Completing the Quilt

1. Sew B to the left side and a Nine-Patch block to the right side of a star block to make a B/Star/Nine-Patch row as shown Figure 5; press seams away from the Star block.

Figure 5

2. Sew a Nine-Patch block to B; press seams toward B.

3. Sew the Nine-Patch/B row to the left side edge and the B/Star/Nine-Patch row to the top of the Angel With Horn block, again referring to Figure 5; press seams toward rows.

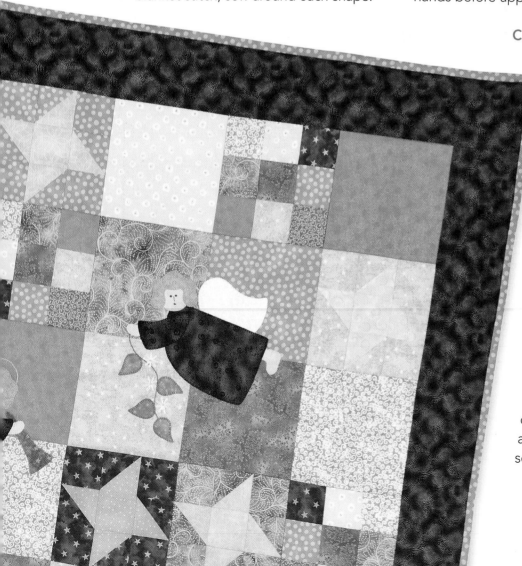

4. Sew a Star block to B to make a B/Star row; press seam toward B. Sew to the right side edge of the Angel With Leaf block as shown in Figure 6; press seam toward Angel block.

Figure 6

5. Join two Star blocks with one Nine-Patch block, again referring to Figure 6; press seams in one direction.

6. Sew the Star/Nine-Patch row to the bottom of the unit pieced in step 4; press seam toward the row.

7. Join the two pieced sections as shown in Figure 7; press seams in one direction.

Figure 7

8. Join two Star blocks with two B squares to make a Star/B unit as shown in Figure 8; press seams toward B and in one direction.

Figure 8

9. Sew the pieced section to the left side edge of the Angel With Heart block, again referring to Figure 8; press seam toward rows.

10. Join two B squares with one each Star and Nine-Patch blocks, again referring to Figure 8; press seams toward B and in one direction.

11. Sew the pieced section to the section pieced in step 9 to complete a row, again referring to Figure 8; press seams toward Angel block.

12. Join three Nine-Patch blocks with two B squares and one Star block to make an X row as shown in Figure 9; press seams in one direction.

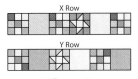

Figure 9

13. Join three B squares with two Nine-Patch blocks and one Star block to make a Y row, again referring to Figure 9; press seams in one direction.

14. Arrange and join the X and Y rows and angel sections as shown in Figure 10 to complete the pieced center; press seams in one direction.

Figure 10

15. Sew a G strip to opposite long sides and H strips to the top and bottom of the pieced center; press seams toward G and H strips.

16. Sandwich the batting between the completed top and prepared backing; pin or baste layers together to hold.

17. Quilt as desired by hand or machine; remove pins or basting. Trim excess backing and batting even with quilt top.

18. Join binding strips on short ends to make one long strip. Fold the strip in half along length with wrong sides together; press.

19. Sew binding to quilt edges, mitering corners and overlapping ends. Fold binding to the back side and stitch in place to finish. ■

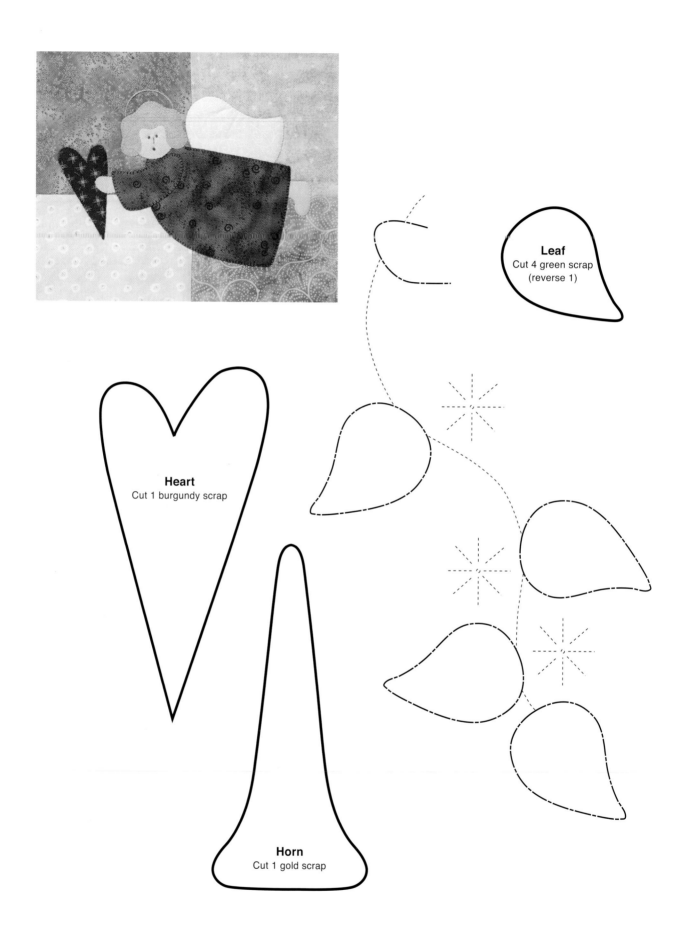

Leaf
Cut 4 green scrap
(reverse 1)

Heart
Cut 1 burgundy scrap

Horn
Cut 1 gold scrap

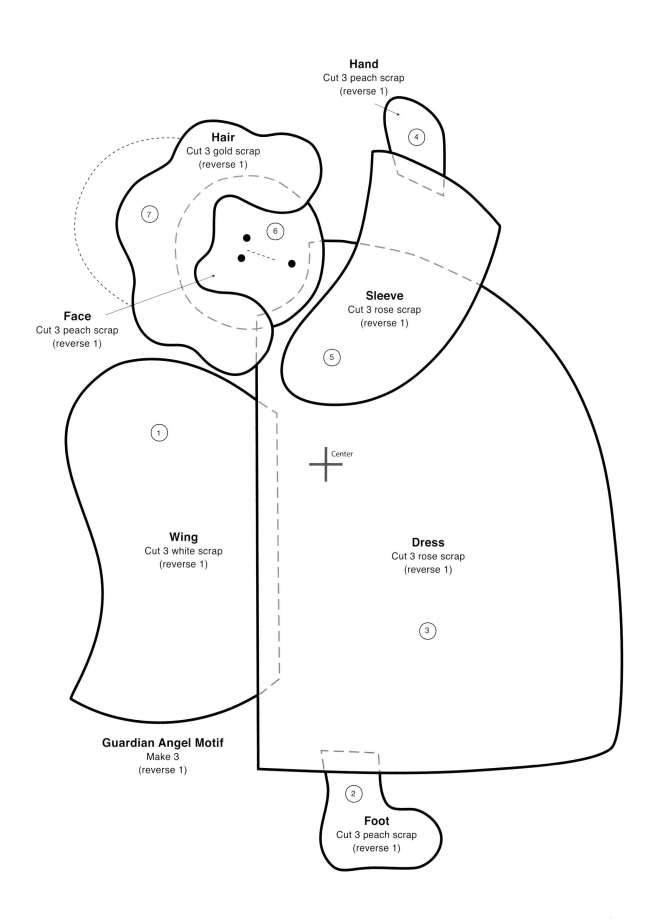

Hand
Cut 3 peach scrap
(reverse 1)

Hair
Cut 3 gold scrap
(reverse 1)

Face
Cut 3 peach scrap
(reverse 1)

Sleeve
Cut 3 rose scrap
(reverse 1)

Center

Wing
Cut 3 white scrap
(reverse 1)

Dress
Cut 3 rose scrap
(reverse 1)

Guardian Angel Motif
Make 3
(reverse 1)

Foot
Cut 3 peach scrap
(reverse 1)

Lord, bless these two as they walk hand in hand down life's road. And when they stub their toes on bumps or potholes, may their strong love for each other keep them from falling. May you be the third member of their partnership from this day forward. Amen.

Wedding Blessing Arm Drape

By Chris Malone

PROJECT SPECIFICATIONS

Skill Level: Advanced
Drape Size: 6" x 32"
Block Size: 6" x 4"
Number of Blocks: 6

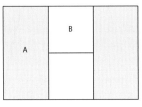

A-B Block
6" x 4"
Make 3

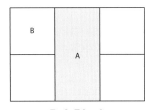

B-A Block
6" x 4"
Make 3

FABRIC Measurements based on 42" usable fabric width.	#STRIPS & PIECES	CUT	#PIECES	SUBCUT
⅛ yard white/ivory tonal 1	1	2½" x 42" B		
¼ yard white/ivory tonal 2	1	2½" x 42" B Appliqué piece as per pattern		
⅓ yard cream tonal	3	2¼" x 42" binding		
⅜ yard white/cream tonal	1	6½" x 8½" C		
	1	2½" x 42"	9	4½" A rectangles
⅜ yard white tulle	1	12" x 38"		
Backing		12" x 38"		

SUPPLIES

- Batting 12" x 38"
- All-purpose thread to match fabric
- White hand-quilting or beading thread
- Scrap light-to-medium weight non-woven interfacing
- 2 yards 1½"-wide ivory wire-edge ribbon
- 1 yard 1½"-wide pale green wire-edge ribbon
- 27 (4mm) cream pearl beads
- 42-46 (4mm) white pearl beads
- Assorted 4mm–15mm glass beads and pearls
- Quilting or beading needle
- Permanent fabric adhesive (optional)
- Basic sewing tools and supplies

INSTRUCTIONS

Completing the Blocks

1. Join two B strips with right sides together along the length; press seams in one direction.

2. Subcut the pieced B strip into nine 2½" B units.

3. Sew a B unit to opposite sides of A to complete a B-A Block as shown in Figure 1; press seams toward A. Repeat to make three B-A Blocks.

Figure 1

Figure 2

4. Sew A to opposite sides of a B unit to complete an A-B Block as shown in Figure 2; press seams toward A. Repeat to make three A-B Blocks.

Completing the Drape

1. Join the A-B Blocks with the B-A blocks, referring to the Placement Diagram for positioning; press seams in one direction.

2. Sew C to the B-A end of the stitched unit to complete the pieced top; press seam toward C.

3. Transfer the heart design to the scrap of interfacing; pin the interfacing to the right side of the white/ivory tonal 2 with pattern on top. Sew all around the pattern lines.

4. Cut out ⅛" from seam; clip curves and trim the tip. Cut a slash through the interfacing only and turn the heart right side out through the opening; press well.

5. Center and hand-stitch the heart shape to C 1" from the top edge to complete the pieced top.

6. Sandwich the batting between the completed top and prepared backing and place the tulle on top; pin or baste layers together to hold.

7. Quilt as desired by hand or machine; remove pins or basting. Trim excess tulle, backing and batting even with quilt top.

8. Join binding strips on short ends to make one long strip. Fold the strip in half along length with wrong sides together; press.

9. Sew binding to quilt edges, mitering corners and overlapping ends. Fold binding to the back side and stitch in place.

10. Use hand-quilting or beading thread to sew a cream pearl to the center of each B square and A rectangle, sewing through all layers.

11. Sew white pearls all around the heart appliqué about ¼" apart, sewing through all layers.

12. To make ribbon roses and buds, cut the ivory ribbon into one 24" length, two 18" lengths and two 6" lengths.

13. Pull ½" of wire from both sides of one end of the 24" ribbon. Twist the ends together to hold as shown in Figure 3.

Figure 3

14. Gently pull the wire from one side only on the opposite end to gather. Continue until entire side is tightly gathered as shown in Figure 4; do not cut wire off.

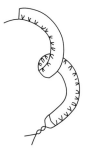

Figure 4

15. To form the rose, hold the twisted end in one hand and start to wrap the gathered ribbon around itself with the other hand. Wrap tightly at first to form a bud, then more loosely to shape an open rose as shown in Figure 5.

Figure 5

16. To end, fold the ends down and wrap the single exposed wire tightly around the base of the rose; trim the excess wires. Use your fingers to shape the rose and pinch the edges until you are satisfied with the look. If desired, use needle and thread to tack the petals in a few places.

17. Repeat steps 13–16 with the 18" lengths to complete two smaller roses.

18. To form each bud, fold the right end of a 6" length down at a right angle as shown in Figure 6; begin to roll this end tightly to the left, forming a round cylinder referring to Figure 7.

Figure 6   **Figure 7**   **Figure 8**

19. Fold the ribbon on the remaining end down toward the back and continue to roll the inner cylinder to the left referring to Figure 8. Again fold the ribbon end down toward the back and roll two more times or until just an inch of ribbon is left.

20. Fold this last inch down into the base of the bud and use a needle and thread to secure the folds.

21. Repeat steps 18–20 to complete two buds; set aside.

22. Cut the pale green ribbon into six 6" lengths. To form each leaf, fold a ribbon length in half so the halves are side by side with raw edges even. Pull the wire from both ends of the same side (inside edge) until completely gathered as shown in Figure 9.

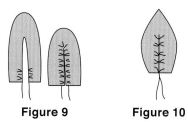

Figure 9   **Figure 10**

23. Twist the wire ends together to hold. Fold and pleat the outside edges together at the base and use needle and matching thread to secure. Pinch the tip of the leaf to shape it as shown in Figure 10.

24. Referring to the project photo and Placement Diagram, arrange the roses and leaves at the bottom of the heart block with the largest rose

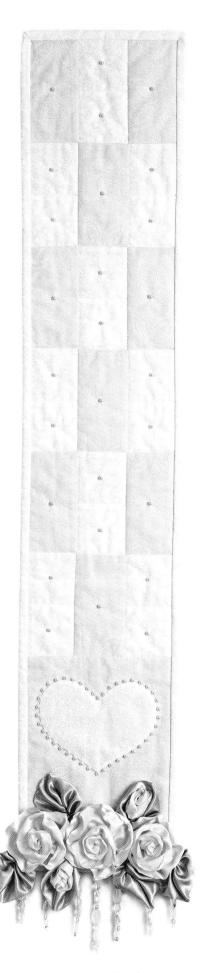

in the center and a smaller rose at each side. Tuck the ends of the leaves under the edges of the roses. Insert the buds between the large and small roses. When satisfied with the arrangement, lift each piece and apply dots of fabric adhesive to secure or tack with needle and thread.

25. To make the bead fringe at the bottom, knot a piece of quilting or beading thread to insert it into the edge of the binding, under the floral embellishments.

26. Starting at one corner, string on an assortment of pearls and glass beads until the fringe measures about 2" in length; end with a small bead. Bring thread around the end bead and insert the needle back into the string of beads; pull needle up the length of the beads and into the edge of the fabric.

27. Make a knot to hold the string and then go through the fabric and come out about 1" away. Repeat the fringe, making it about 2½" long. Space the next fringe 1¼" away and about 2½" long. The center fringe is ¾" away and 3" long. Repeat the sequence to the other end. ◼

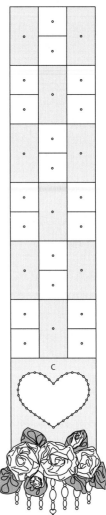

Wedding Blessing Arm Drape
Placement Diagram
6" x 32"

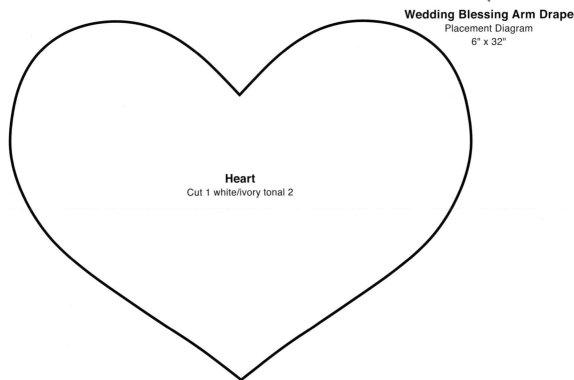

Heart
Cut 1 white/ivory tonal 2

Calla Lily Shawl

Continued from page 31.

Center Quilting Design

Annie's® Published by Annie's, 306 East Parr Road, Berne, IN 46711. Printed in USA. Copyright © 2019 Annie's. All rights reserved. This publication may not be reproduced in part or in whole without written permission from the publisher.

RETAIL STORES: If you would like to carry this publication or any other Annie's publication, visit AnniesWSL.com.

Every effort has been made to ensure that the instructions in this publication are complete and accurate. We cannot, however, take responsibility for human error, typographical mistakes or variations in individual work. Please visit AnniesCustomerService.com to check for pattern updates.

ISBN: 978-1-64025-094-9

1 2 3 4 5 6 7 8 9